UNDERSTANDING THE IMPORTANCE OF INFORMATION

Beth A. Pulver and Donald C. Adcock

Heinemann Library
Chicago, Illinois

© 2009 Heinemann Library
an imprint of Capstone Global Library,LLC
Chicago, Illinois

Customer Service 888-454-2279
Visit our website at www.heinemannraintree.com

Design: Richard Parker and Tinstar Design Ltd.
Photo research: Fiona Orbell and Elizabeth Alexander

Origination by Chroma Graphics (Overseas) Pte. Ltd.
Printed and bound in China by Leo Paper Products Ltd

ISBN: 978-1-4329-1230-7 (hc)

13 12 11
10 9 8 7 6 5 4 3 2

Library of Congress Cataloging-in-Publication Data
Pulver, Beth A.
  Understanding the importance of information / Beth A. Pulver and Donald C. Adcock.
     p. cm. -- (Information literacy skills)
  Includes bibliographical references and index.
  ISBN 978-1-4329-1230-7
  1. Information literacy--Juvenile literature. 2. Information behavior--Juvenile literature. 3. Freedom of information--Juvenile literature. 4. Freedom of expression--Juvenile literature. I. Adcock, Donald C. II. Title.
  ZA3080.P855 2008
  028.7--dc22
                    2008019419

Acknowledgments
The author and publishers are grateful to the following for permission to reproduce copyright material: © UK edition of "Memoirs of a Teenage Amnesiac" by Gabrielle Zevin, Bloomsbury Publishing Plc. p. **30**; © Alamy pp. /Blend Images **10**, /david pearson **17**; © Corbis pp. /Jeffry W. Myers **37**, /Ed Kashi **19**, /Henry Diltz **29**, /Jonathan Brady/epa **41**, /Reuters **21**, /Underwood & Underwood **4**; © Getty Images pp. /Akhtar Hussein/Liaison Agency **26**, /Bruce Laurance **23**, /Colorblind Images **5**, /Indranil Mukherjee/AFP **12**, /Ron Chapple/Taxi **11**, /Valerie Macon/AFP **39**; © Photodisc pp. **9**, **38**; © Photolibrary/Digital Vision **32**; © The Library of Congress **6**.

Background features and cover photograph reproduced with permission of © iStockphoto.

Every effort has been made to contact copyright holders of any material reproduced in this book. Any omissions will be rectified in subsequent printings if notice is given to the publishers.

Contents

The Importance of Information 4

The Right to Information 8

Why Is Equal Access to Information Important? .. 16

Students and Information 22

The Responsibilities of Free Expression 25

The Internet and Freedom of Information 38

Summary 40

The Bill of Rights... 42

Glossary 44

Find Out More 46

Further Research.. 47

Index... 48

Some words are shown in bold, **like this.** You can find the definitions for these words in the glossary.

The Importance of Information

Every day you receive thousands of pieces of information. Your parents, friends, and teachers all give you information. You read books, watch TV, surf the Web, play video games, and listen to music. You are potentially getting information from all of these activities.

If you have a question, whether it's something you want to know for your own interest or a class assignment, you have the ability to research it in a number of places. Much of your research can be done very quickly **online** or in a library. If you don't have a book, you can find it at your school library, the public library, or a bookstore. If you can't get to any of those places, you can order it online without leaving your house.

With all these sources of information available, you probably take it for granted that you have the right to access information. In other places in the world, people do not have such access to information. In some countries the government limits the information people are allowed to have. In some places, even in this country, lack of technology, money, and other resources limit the information available.

In this book we will look at how our country's government and history support our right to information, and some of the responsibilities that come with the rights we have.

Andrew Carnegie is sometimes referred to as the Patron Saint of Libraries.

Today libraries offer a variety of services, ranging from storytime for small children to providing tax forms for adults. They also provide computer and Internet access for many people.

Libraries and information

Thomas Jefferson, Benjamin Franklin, and other founders of the United States believed that an educated public was necessary for a **democratic** society. They thought that in order for people to make good decisions, they needed to have all the information possible.

Libraries are an important part of accessible information. A free library means that all members of a community have the same access to information, regardless of wealth. The first town library was founded in 1636 in Boston, Massachusetts. The Boston Public Library still exists today.

Many libraries in the United States were built with money donated by Scottish-American businessman Andrew Carnegie (1823–1929). Money from Carnegie built over 2,000 libraries around the world. Over 1,000 were built in the United States, 660 in Great Britain and Ireland, 156 in Canada, and several others around the world. Many of these libraries still stand today.

Types of libraries

There are many different kinds of libraries. A school library usually contains books at the right reading level for the students at the school. Your school library probably has fiction as well as nonfiction books. Your library may also have computers and other resources. Usually only students from the school are allowed to use the school library or borrow books from it.

Today, with online catalogs, you can access libraries without leaving your home.

Public libraries

A public library is usually run by a town or city. Most towns think it is important that their residents have access to information. Everyone is welcome at a public library, but usually only residents of the city or nearby cities can borrow books. Sometimes only residents of the city or nearby cities can use library resources like computers. A public library may have a wide variety of fiction and nonfiction books, DVDs, CDs, and magazines. Some of these materials will be appropriate for you, but others will be too complicated or adult for your needs.

Some public libraries may have a special children's area with comfortable chairs, and even toys. Some public libraries have programs that have authors and speakers who give presentations on topics like gardening or other hobbies. Some also have "Book Buddy" programs where older boys and girls can volunteer to read to young children. Many public libraries have special programs, such as book readings or town meetings. Public libraries have all these resources because they exist to provide services to the residents of the town.

Special libraries

If you have a school project about architecture, you might check out a book about the architect Frank Lloyd Wright. You can probably find biographies of him, as well as books about his buildings, in your school or public library.

Imagine that you are a historian studying architecture. You don't want to just read what other people say about Wright, you want to look at his building plans yourself. You may even want to view his business contracts or other personal papers. This information may not be in a public library. It will probably be at a special library attached to a museum, or in a college or university library. Many famous people donate such papers to a specific library for researchers to use in the future.

In a regular library you can wander around looking at different books, but in many special libraries you have to ask the librarian for the book you want, and he or she brings it to you. These special libraries often have very valuable books that they need to keep safe for future research.

College and university libraries

Colleges and universities have very large libraries with thousands and thousands of books. They also have large collections of journals related to the courses taught at the college. The major function of the libraries at colleges and universities is to provide the resources and assistance needed by the students and the professors who are conducting research. They may have a small collection of fiction books to read for pleasure, but the literature collection is provided for research purposes rather than reading pleasure. Many college and university libraries allow anyone to use their resources in the library, but only allow their students and teachers to borrow things from it.

Whatever kind of library you are using, the best way to find what you need is to start with a librarian.

The Right to Information

As citizens of the United States, we have certain rights guaranteed to us by the United States Constitution. Some of these rights pertain to the right to information. The U.S. Constitution became the law of the land in 1787. The first ten amendments, or changes, were made between 1789 and 1791, and are known as the Bill of Rights (see p.42).

The Declaration of Independence says that certain rights are "inalienable." The word *inalienable* means that you cannot alienate, or separate, the right from the person. This means that the writers of the Declaration, and the Constitution, thought that people should have certain rights no matter where they live in the world. It is important to understand that not everyone agrees that certain rights are inalienable. The right to freedom of information is not the same in different countries and cultures.

The First Amendment

Congress shall make no law respecting an establishment of religion, or prohibiting the free exercise thereof; or abridging the freedom of speech, or of the press; or the right of the people peaceably to assemble, and to petition the government for a redress of grievances.

Freedom of speech

The First Amendment has two statements that are important to the right to information. The first says that the government cannot abridge, or reduce, people's right to the freedom of speech. This means that in the United States you cannot be arrested for speaking your mind, even if what you say is in disagreement with the government. This amendment is important to gaining information because it means people can write books or make speeches that contradict what the government says. This means information is not controlled by the government.

Limits on free speech

Just because you have the legal right to speak your mind doesn't mean that you can say whatever you want. You can still get in trouble with your parents, friends, or teachers. There are other limits to the right as well. You are not allowed to lie about people. You may not make false statements about a person that might ruin the person's

Gossip is not protected under your right to free speech.

reputation. This is called **slander**. If you make up a story about someone and publish it in the newspaper, you can be sued for **libel**. You are also not allowed to say things for the purpose of causing a disturbance or riot. You may have heard the expression "Like shouting fire in a crowded theater." This refers to the fact that if you stood up in a crowded place and shouted "fire" just to see what would happen, you could be arrested. This is because shouting "fire" can cause a stampede, and people can get hurt.

Freedom of the press

The second part of the amendment that is important to our topic is the freedom of the press. In many countries the government controls the press. This means they own the newspapers and, in some cases, TV stations as well. In some countries the government may also try to control the Internet. They do this by blocking websites. Internet blocking is not just used by countries. Individuals, companies, schools, and libraries can purchase software that prevents people from seeing all websites.

Freedom of the press means that newspapers and magazines can publish stories even if the government doesn't want them to. In some countries, a newspaper reporter can be arrested for writing stories that are antigovernment. Like the freedom of speech, freedom of the press makes it easier for the public to get information.

In the United States, the freedom of the press protects all forms of news information.

Limits on press freedom

There are limits to the freedom of the press. Just like with freedom of speech, newspapers are not allowed to publish untrue stories. During times of war, there may be other restrictions placed on newspapers. Because middle-school and high-school students are not adults, there may be more restrictions placed on their rights to freedom of speech and freedom of the press.

In the United States and many other countries, issues of freedom of speech and the press are often decided in courts.

Court cases

In 1968, three students were suspended from high school for wearing black armbands. The students wore these armbands to protest the United States' involvement in the Vietnam War. In 1969, the **Supreme Court** ruled that wearing the armbands was protected under freedom of speech. This case is known as Tinker v. Des Moines Independent Community School District.

In 1983, some students wrote a special section of the school newspaper dealing with teen pregnancy and divorce. The school principal objected to the section and **censored** it. In 1988, the Supreme Court ruled that since the newspaper was part of a class, it was not a public forum. The principal had the right to decide what could and could not go in the student newspaper. This case is known as Hazelwood School District v. Kuhlmeir.

Both of these cases involved students in public schools. This means that in some ways the schools are part of the state government. Students at private schools, which are not supported by the government, may have fewer protections when it comes to freedom of speech and freedom of the press. Students at public universities and colleges tend to have more rights when it comes to freedom of speech and freedom of the press.

It is important to remember that the Bill of Rights states what the government can and cannot prevent you from doing.

Other First-Amendment protections

The First Amendment does not just protect political speech. It also protects people's rights to perform, paint, or say things that other people simply do not like or might find offensive. It also protects other forms of communication, for example bumper stickers, lawn signs, or the armbands discussed. The First Amendment protects a person's right to create unpopular works. It does not mean that a specific store, museum, or person has to sell or display the item.

Is it censorship?

Newspapers cannot publish every story. Many stories are not well written, lack supporting proof, or would not be of interest to the newspaper's readership. There is not enough room in a newspaper or magazine to include every story. Editors and publishers are allowed to make decisions about what does and does not go in a newspaper or magazine.

Libraries and schools cannot afford to buy every book. Teachers, principals, and librarians all have to make decisions about what books they should and should not purchase for the school. They purchase books that are related to the subjects taught in the schools. Censorship and book banning does not refer to public places or businesses making reasonable decisions about what books they will and will not own.

Book banning

Despite your right to information, there are groups of people who wish to restrict access to materials. These groups often petition libraries and school boards to remove or restrict the access to printed materials in their collections.

Groups sometimes try to keep others from reading books they do not approve of.

In this situation, a person or group of people believe that they should decide for others what they can and cannot read. This happens most frequently in schools and public libraries. There have been many court cases involving groups who wished to censor, or ban, a book from a school or library. In most cases the group believes the book is offensive or harmful to students.

The American Library Association's ten most challenged books of 2006

Book	Complaint
And Tango Makes Three	Homosexuality, antifamily, unsuited to age group
Gossip Girls (series)	Homosexuality, sexual content, language, drug use, unsuited to age group
Alice (series)	Offensive language, sexual content
The Earth, My Butt, and Other Big Round Things	Sexual content, antifamily, offensive language, and unsuited to age group
The Bluest Eye	Sexual content, offensive language, unsuited to age group
Scary Stories	Occult/satanism, insensitivity, unsuited to age group, violence
Athletic Shorts	Offensive language, homosexuality
The Perks of Being a Wallflower	Homosexuality, sexually explicit, offensive language, unsuited to age group
Beloved (Winner 1988 Pulitzer Prize)	Offensive language, sexual content, and unsuited to age group
The Chocolate War	Sexual content, offensive language, violence

Other frequently protested books include the classics *Adventures of Huckleberry Finn, Catcher in the Rye*, and *Of Mice and Men.*

Freedom of Information Act

In 1966, the Freedom of Information Act (FOIA) was made law. The FOIA says that U.S. citizens have the right to information the government has. Any person or institution, such as a newspaper or university, can request information. In 1974, after a government scandal, the law was rewritten to make government agencies do a better job of obeying the law. In 1996, the law was changed again to make access to electronic information easier. In 2001, shortly after the September 11 attacks in New York and Washington, D.C., the act was further changed. Many people believe the September 11, 2001 attacks were used as an excuse for limiting access to information under the FOIA.

Under the FOIA, it is assumed that the person requesting information has a right to the information. If the government does not want to provide the information, it needs to prove why the information cannot or should not be provided. Just because a person has the right to information under the FOIA does not mean that the information is free. There is often a fee associated with obtaining the requested information.

There are certain exceptions to the FOIA, including the office of the president. The FOIA is important to newspapers trying to write stories about government officials or policies. It is also important for individuals trying to research their own records, and historians trying to write about past events.

Other countries

Other countries also have Freedom of Information Acts. Sweden's Freedom of the Press Act (1766) is thought to be the oldest. The United Kingdom's FOIA became law in 2000. Over 100,000 requests are made each year, most of them from private citizens. Many countries are currently developing similar laws. Groups around the world that campaign for more freedom of information participate each year in "Right to Know Day," sponsored by the Freedom of Information Advocates Network.

A sample FOIA request letter

Agency Head <i>(or Freedom of Information Act Officer)</i>
Name of Agency
Address of Agency
City, State, Zip Code

Re: Freedom of Information Act Request

Dear *(Name of the FOIA Officer as listed on the agency's website)*:

This is a request under the Freedom of Information Act 5 U.S.C. § 552.

I request that a copy of the following documents *(or documents containing the following information)* be provided to me: *(identify the documents or information as specifically as possible.)*

In order to help to determine my status to assess fees, you should know I am *(insert a suitable description of the requester and the purpose of the request.)*

(For example: In order to help to determine my status to assess fees, you should know I am)

a representative of the news media affiliated with the _____ *(newspaper, magazine, describe publication contract or describe past publication history)*, and this request is made for purposes of gathering news and not for commercial use.

affiliated with _____, an educational or noncommercial scientific institution, and this request is made for a scholarly or scientific purpose and not for commercial use.

an individual seeking information for personal use and not for commercial use.

affiliated with a private corporation and am seeking information for use in the company's business.

I am willing to pay fees for this request up to a maximum of $_____. If you estimate that the fees will exceed this limit, please inform me first.

(Optional) I request a waiver of all fees for this request. Disclosure of the requested information to me is in the public interest because it is likely to contribute significantly to public understanding of the operations or activities of the government and is not primarily in my commercial interest. *(Include a specific explanation.)*

If you deny any part of this request, please cite each specific reason that you think justifies your refusal to release the information and notify me of appeal procedures available to me under the law.

If you have any questions processing this request, you may contact me at the following telephone number or e-mail address: *(number and address)*. Thank you for your consideration of my request.

Sincerely,

Name
Address
City, State, Zip Code
Telephone Number *(Optional)*

Taken from: http://www.gwu.edu/~nsarchiv/nsa/foia/guide.html#requests

Why Is Equal Access to Information Important?

As the saying goes, "Knowledge IS Power." This is why nondemocratic countries often try to limit the amount of information people have.

The founders of the United States knew that if the country they were trying to start was going to succeed, the people would have to be well informed. Otherwise how could they participate in the decisions of the government? Information is needed not only for political decisions, but for everyday decisions as well. There are many things that can limit a person's access to information, including poverty and location. People in rural locations may be limited by a lack of electricity or libraries. Communities that have people living in poverty may have libraries and schools that are not funded well enough to provide access to many books and computers.

Consumer rights

Having limited access to information can cause a person to make bad decisions, or prevent a person from getting further ahead in life. Consider a young woman purchasing her first car. She needs to know what type of car she can afford that has the best gas mileage and safety record. She must also find out about automobile insurance. She wants to know which company offers the best coverage at a rate she can afford. Then she must find out the amount of the taxes to be paid and the fees for license plates. All this requires hours of research and access to the information in order for the young woman to make her decision.

Recommendations and evaluations

Unfortunately, there are dishonest organizations and businesses. There are businesses that take money for services they do not perform. There are even fake charities that solicit money from people. It is important to carefully evaluate an organization or business before giving it money. In the United States, the website Charity Navigator can help you evaluate a charity before you give it money. Websites such as the Better Business Bureau and Angie's List keep track of consumer complaints so that you can evaluate a business.

One of the first steps in getting information about a business may be simply to talk to people you know. If you belong to a listserve or other online social group, you can post a message asking for opinions. You can also talk to people you know. This type of resource has a downside though. It is now very easy to spread false information about a business. For a small business this can be devastating.

Without the proper information, this woman could make a bad and expensive decision about her purchase. A skillful salesperson will hopefully help the customer with the information needed.

Health care

Access to information can make a difference for a person with a medical condition. Today, because of the Internet, people who are not medical professionals have access to a wide variety of medical information. This can be both positive and negative. On the positive side, people can learn more about their medical conditions. They can join online support groups and talk to others with the same condition. If they are unhappy with their doctor, they can try to find a new doctor or more information online.

On the negative side, medical information can be difficult for nonprofessionals to understand. People may misdiagnose themselves based on information they do not understand. A person may decide he or she does not need to see a doctor, or does not trust the doctor, because of something read online. When doing medical research, it is important to only use trustworthy sites and to discuss your findings with your doctor.

Voting

Access to information is important to voters during national elections. Without access to information, citizens of countries, cities, or villages would not be able to have an educated say in their government. In a democratic country, it is important that there be information from a variety of sources. We have access to information about new laws and policies made by the government, interactions of our country with other countries, and how elected officials are voting on issues. Without access to information, you would not know how candidates for office feel on subjects like wars, taxes, health care, immigration, and the environment. Without access to information, there are many things that you would not be able to learn. All of this information means that you also have a responsibility to stay informed about the issues that are important where you live.

Gaining skills

The amount of information may sometimes seem overwhelming. But you already have many of the skills you need to evaluate and use this information. Let's say you only have enough money to buy one CD this month. Your two favorite artists are both coming out with new releases. How do you decide which one to buy? Your best friend gives you an opinion, but you still aren't sure. You decide to do some research. You can read reviews in music magazines, read online reviews, or visit the music store and discuss it with the people working there. Even everyday purchases such as this can be a good way to practice your research and evaluation skills.

The skill of evaluating information can be useful in all walks of life. These stockbrokers and traders often need to make quick decisions based on information that changes by the minute.

Government use of information

Individuals and businesses are not the only ones who need information. Governments need accurate information about their citizens and lands. Without this information, how would a state know where to build new schools, parks, and hospitals? Politicians need information about how people feel about issues so that they can enact fair laws and represent voters' interests.

Censuses

One of the main ways a government gains information about its people is by conducting a census. A census is simply the counting of people in a specific area. The United Nations recommends that countries conduct a survey every ten years by mail or by going door to door. The United States began conducting such surveys in 1790. The information gathered helps governments make decisions and predictions about the future. The U.S. census is also used to assign the number of seats a state has in Congress.

Individuals and businesses have the right to view census information. This can help you if you are trying to do research about your family.

Privacy

Although the government needs to collect information about its citizens, individuals also have a right to privacy. The government needs to know how many people live in your house. However, it does not need to know what you talk about, where you go, what you eat, or what you think. Businesses also do not have the right to access all of your personal information.

It is important that you protect your right to privacy. This is one reason you should never give out personal information online. Many times websites will ask you to fill out surveys or answer questions. When you do this, you are giving information to the business running the site. You should always discuss such surveys with a trusted adult before filling them out.

Sometimes when you make a purchase at a store, you may be asked to give your zip code or phone number. Stores do this to help track where their customers live. However, if you give your phone number to a store clerk, you may be allowing the store to call you or sell your phone number to others.

Countries around the world gather information about their citizens to use when making decisions. China employed more than 6 million census workers for its last nationwide census, in 2000. They gathered information about the country's population of 1.3 billion people.

Identity theft

One of the biggest security issues today is identity theft. This is when a person steals your personal information, such as your address, birthday, and social security number. The person can then use this information to open credit cards in your name. The thief never pays for the purchases made in your name. It can take years to solve the problems created by identity theft. In the meantime, it may be difficult for you to obtain credit, or even get a job.

Students and Information

As discussed before, children and students also have the right to information. Schools need to develop programs that provide access to information and teach students how to use the information. There are two documents that are important in helping schools do this, the **Library Bill of Rights** and the *Standards for the 21st Century Learner*.

The Library Bill of Rights

The purpose of the Library Bill of Rights is to help schools develop policies that provide physical and intellectual access to information. The American Library Association adopted the Library Bill of Rights in 1948 and reaffirmed it in 1996. It states that "all libraries are forums for information and ideas," that, "books and other library resources should be provided to the people of the community the library serves, that materials should not be excluded because of the origin, or views of those who created it," and that "libraries should provide materials and information presenting all points of view on current and historical issues." Finally, it states that a person's origin, age, background, or views should not be used to deny access to library resources.

One of the purposes of the Library Bill of Rights is to provide guidelines for libraries to use when developing policies and procedures related to the selection of materials. Since its adoption there have been many interpretations of the Library Bill of Rights. These deal with such issues as access for children and young adults to nonprint materials, access to resources and services in the school library media program, and economic barriers to information access. Access to resources and services in the school library media program is often referred to as the School Library Bill of Rights.

The Library Bill of Rights

The Library Bill of Rights states that

- All libraries are forums for information and ideas.
- Books and other library resources should be provided to the people of the community the library serves.
- Materials should not be excluded because of the origin, or views of those who created it.
- Libraries should provide materials and information presenting all points of view on current and historical issues.
- A person's origin, age, background, or views should not be used to deny access to the library's resources.

Adopted by the American Library Association in 1948 and reaffirmed in 1996.

Standards for the 21st Century Learner

School libraries use both the Library Bill of Rights and a set of standards for student learning. The standards for learning are statements of what skills students should have in order to access, evaluate, and use information. According to the *Standards for the 21st Century Learner*, the skills learners need in order to use information resources and tools are the ability to:

- inquire, think critically, and gain knowledge
- draw conclusions, make informed decisions, apply knowledge to new situations, and create new knowledge
- share knowledge and participate ethically and productively as members of our democratic society
- pursue personal and aesthetic growth.

In addition to having these skills, learners will develop behaviors that will make them independent researchers, investigators, and problem solvers. Learners will also develop beliefs and attitudes that will guide their thinking and intellectual behavior.

This 21st-century learner will develop behaviors that will make her an independent researcher, investigator, and problem solver.

The *Standards for the 21st Century Learner* also state that a school library should provide to all students "equitable access to books and reading, to information, and to information technology in an environment that is safe and conducive to learning." School library collections should be developed and evaluated to support the school's curriculum and to meet the diverse learning needs of students. Just like public libraries, school libraries were founded on the basis of providing access to information to everyone. The right of access to information is an important intellectual freedom.

Although there are many school and public libraries, some students still do not have access to information. Not every community has a public library. Not every school has a school library. There are people who live in areas so remote that Internet access is not available. There are also places around the world where the government and politicians believe that not everyone is entitled to equal access to information.

What does a modern library provide?

- Books, books, and more books
- Homework and reference help
- Services for children and parents
- Government forms
- Internet access
- Gathering place for kids, teens, and adults
- Art exhibits
- Classes
- Sometimes even a coffee shop

The Responsibilities of Free Expression

As we discussed, freedom of expression is a right protected by the First Amendment of the Bill of Rights. This amendment to the United States Constitution guarantees the right to express yourself freely in speech, writing, art, and clothing. This right is just as important as your right to access information. The right to free expression allows authors to write the information they think is important and have it printed, so that everyone can read it and learn from it. This right is given to everyone so that the exchange of ideas can be made freely. As citizens of a free society with an elected government, the right of free expression gives us the ability to make informed decisions about the election of government officials and government policy. With this right, however, comes great responsibility.

Your speech is protected, but this does not mean that you can say anything about anyone. Legally you are not allowed to speak false statements that might ruin a person's reputation. This is called slander. You are also not allowed to write false statements that might ruin a person's reputation. This is called libel. Both libel and slander are making false statements about a person, but one is done in speaking and one is done in writing. Both libel and slander are against the law.

The definition of slander and libel

The right to free expression does not include the right to make false statements about a person.

- Slander is when you make a false statement about a person that might ruin that person's reputation. This statement is made orally.

- Libel is when you make a false statement in writing about a person that might ruin that person's reputation.

- Both slander and libel are against the law.

A famous slander case

Oprah Winfrey has been a famous talk-show host for years. Her TV show is very popular, and she is seen as someone who can influence many people.

In April 1996, Oprah had people representing the beef industry and a vegetarian activist on her show. There had recently been an outbreak of "Mad Cow" disease in the United Kingdom, and many people had concerns about the safety of eating beef. The two debated about the safety of beef. As a result of the debate, Oprah Winfrey said that she would not eat hamburgers anymore.

In the state of Texas, there is a special law that allows people to sue for libel or slander on behalf of a food or agricultural product. The cattle industry claimed that Oprah's comments caused beef prices to fall dramatically. The courts ruled that, in fact, Oprah had not uttered any false statements. Oprah's right to free speech gave her the right to state her opinion about eating beef. After the trial, Oprah was quoted as saying, "Free speech not only lives, it rocks!"

Oprah Winfrey stands outside a Texas courthouse in 1998. What constitutes libel can be difficult to decide and may have to be determined in a court of law. The financial penalties for libel can be huge, but so can the costs of going to court.

Ironically, Oprah herself is often accused of limiting free speech. This is because she asks her employees to sign a very strict contract, which prevents them from discussing or writing about Oprah for the rest of their lives.

Your responsibility

Today, with the Internet, it is very easy to spread false information. If you send an e-mail to a friend with a piece of gossip, that e-mail can be passed around the school before class starts the next day. You must think very carefully before putting information online. This is true of your personal information as well. If you put information on Facebook, MySpace, or other sites, many people can view it. This includes your parents, teachers, and future employers. Once information is posted online, it never really goes away. There have been cases of people losing jobs because of e-mails they sent. There have even been cases of people losing spots on sports teams and job offers because of information found on sites such as MySpace.

The right to gather

Related to your right to free speech is your right to gather as a group to discuss or protest issues. Those who have opinions different from yours also have this same right. This right also must be used with responsibility. You may need to ask permission to use a certain space or date and time to hold your protest. You are not allowed to encourage your group or other groups to start a riot or fight with others who do not share your opinion.

As mentioned earlier, it is also good to be careful generally and not spread too much personal information around to too many people. Identity theft is a growing concern around the world. Computers assist us in many ways, but technology has also made it easier for criminals to steal people's identities and money.

Copyright laws

Protecting authors' free speech goes farther than allowing them to publish their ideas and opinions. It also means protecting those words, ideas, and opinions from being stolen. This protection is provided by the **copyright** law. The copyright law clearly says that an author's literary, artistic, musical, and dramatic piece of work is protected by the law. This means that in order to use it, you must ask the author's permission. It also means that you may not make copies or distribute duplicate copies to others. Artwork, the choreography of a dance, music, plays, and the staging of where the actors stand when performing the play are also protected by copyright law.

That means that you cannot perform another person's drama, music, or choreography without his or her permission. Pieces of art like paintings, sculptures, drawings, and photographs may not be copied or distributed to others. Musical works, including the lyrics and music, are protected by copyright law. When you make a copy of your favorite compact disc to give to a friend, you may be in violation of the copyright law.

A famous copyright case

George Harrison was a member of the music group the Beatles. In 1970 he came out with a solo album. One of the songs, "My Sweet Lord," was about Harrison's religious feelings. The song became a number-one hit. Many people thought the song sounded similar to a song from the 1960s, "He's So Fine."

Harrison admitted that he had heard "He's So Fine" before, but said he had written his song independently, and that the two songs were different. The judge eventually found that while Harrison did not intend to copy "He's So Fine," the two songs were almost identical. Harrison was found guilty of breaking the copyright laws. He took someone else's work, performed it as his own, and made money from it. Copyright law does not require that someone intentionally copy a song in order for it to be illegal. Money was awarded to the owner of the rights to "He's So Fine."

Today, sampling is a popular music technique. Sampling refers to when an artist intentionally borrows a section from a famous song and includes it as part of his or her own song. People have different opinions as to whether sampling is a violation of copyright law or an example of **fair use**.

In the early 1970s, George Harrison was sued because his song "My Sweet Lord" sounded like a song by the Chiffons, "He's So Fine." The judge ruled that Harrison had unintentionally copied the earlier song and had broken the law.

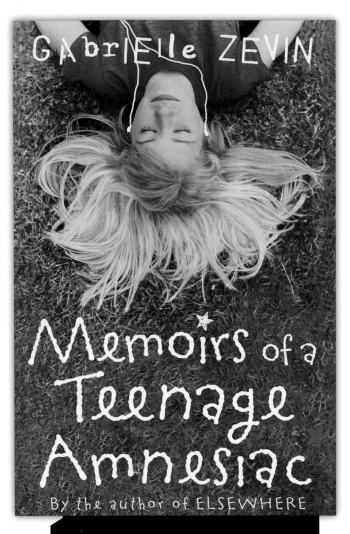

GAbriElle ZEVIN

Memoirs of a Teenage Amnesiac

By the author of ELSEWHERE

It would be illegal to put the text of
this novel into this book, but using this
picture is considered fair use.

Fair use

If you want to copy pages out of the encyclopedia to continue your
research at home, you are not in violation of the copyright law. This is
different than copying a compact disc, because you are using a small part
of the whole book for research. This is allowed because of an exception
in the law. This exception is called fair use. Fair use allows you to make
copies of certain amounts of text, audio, or video for research and for
education or discussion.

Amount of information allowed under fair use

Text
- Can copy up to 10% or 10,000 words, whichever is less
- Poems less than 250 words, only 3 poems per poet

Motion
- Can copy up to 10% or 3 minutes, whichever is less

Music, Sound
- Up to 10% but not more than 30 seconds

Video
- Up to 10% but not more than 3 minutes

Illustrations/Photos
- No more than 5 images by an artist, or 10% or 15 images from a published collected work, whichever is less

The Harry Potter books by author J.K. Rowling have been very popular for years. In 2008, Rowling sued a librarian who wanted to publish a lexicon, or encyclopedia, of the books. Rowling claimed that the lexicon violated her copyright. The librarian claimed that the material used in the encyclopedia fell under the rules of fair use. Interestingly, the librarian first developed a fan website with the same information. Rowling did not object to the website, and even praised it, before the author tried to publish the information as a book.

Technology today

Today's technology, such as the Internet, databases, CD and DVD burners, digital video files, and digital sound files, make it very easy to violate the copyright law. When you make copies and then sell or distribute the copies, you are in violation of the copyright law. This is called **piracy**. When you purchase a CD or a sound file, it is for your use only. Copying the CD or a song from the CD and transferring that file to someone else's music player is illegal. However, it is legal to borrow CDs, books, and videos from a library.

Plagiarism

Just as you have the right to read works written by a variety of authors, the authors have the right to own and protect their work. **Plagiarism** is another word for cheating by copying. When you commit plagiarism, you submit someone else's ideas or words as your own.

Many people do this accidentally. They copy phrases or sentences from a book or article, forget where they found the work, and put it in their own paper. Other people incorrectly believe that if they have changed the words around, they have not committed plagiarism.

Catching plagiarism

Your teacher has many ways of discovering if you have copied your paper. If your work does not seem like it was written by you, your teacher will probably become suspicious. If you have copied from another student, past or present, the teacher may recognize the work or may ask other teachers if they recognize it. If you copy from a published source or something you find online, your teacher may type a few sentences into a search engine and discover that you have copied the work.

Most schools have codes of conduct with rules against plagiarizing. In some schools and colleges, plagiarizing could lead to you being expelled or unable to graduate.

Most schools have codes of conduct with rules against plagiarizing. The penalties may mean you fail the assignment or even the class. In some schools and colleges, you may be expelled, or kicked out, of school for plagiarizing, even if you do so accidentally. Adults have lost their jobs and the respect of other people for committing plagiarism.

How to avoid plagiarizing

Take careful notes:
- Make sure you take notes as you read. Write down where you read something and what page it was on.
- If you copy a quotation from a book, make sure to mark it as a quotation.

Give credit where credit is due:
- If you agree with something you read in book, you can use a phrase such as "As Jane Austen says. . . ." This lets the reader know whose idea the thought is.
- When writing your **bibliography** and footnotes, include more than is strictly necessary.

Use quotation marks:
- If you are quoting from a source, use quotation marks and make sure the sentence includes the information about where you read the quote.

Protect yourself:
- Make sure to give yourself enough time to complete your assignments, that way you won't be tempted to take shortcuts.
- Keep drafts of your paper. Sometimes a student may be unfairly accused of plagiarizing. If you have copies of your notes and earlier drafts of your paper, you can prove that the thoughts are your own.

Citations

A bibliography, **footnotes**, and **endnotes** all help you avoid committing plagiarism. As you are doing your research, it is important to make sure you list all of the sources of your information. This list of sources will remind you which sources you might have paraphrased from or quoted to use in your presentation.

The list will also become your bibliography, or list of works **cited**. A bibliography is a list of each source used during research. Each citation for a type of source has its own way to be written, but all contain basic information, including the author, title, place of publication, publisher, and date of publication. Some source types, like encyclopedia articles, magazine articles, and Web pages, require additional information for their entry in the bibliography.

Footnotes and endnotes

Footnotes are notes placed at the bottom of the page. The note refers to a source of information and includes the page number within the source where the quote or paraphrase came from. When you see a number slightly above the last letter of a word, you will know that there is a footnote. An example might be if you read "bibliography.[1]" The number "1" would normally indicate that there is a note at the end of the page also labeled "1" that is related to a quote or paraphrase about a bibliography.

Endnotes also cite quotes or paraphrases used within the text of a presentation, but instead of being noted at the bottom of the page, they are placed at the end of the written presentation, and each note is in numerical order of use. Both footnotes and endnotes are another way to show that you have used information from reliable sources, and that the information is not your original work. Even though you have used footnotes or endnotes, you must also still have a bibliography, or list of works cited, included with your presentation.

Today, many computer programs can help you create or manage footnotes or endnotes. Most word-processing programs, such as Microsoft Word, can do this. Professional researchers and writers often use programs designed specifically to keep track of citations and merge them into the main document.

A bibliography organizer

Create a grid, like this one, as your bibliography organizer. Fill in each section of the organizer as you use each information source. You will use this organizer to create your bibliography.

	Author	Source 1	Source 2	Source 3
Title of magazine, newspaper, or book				
Title of article				
Title of Web page				
Volume number				
Page numbers				
Place of publication				
Publisher				
Copyright or update year				
Web address				
Date you first used website				

Fraud

As previously discussed, freedom of speech does not give you the right to lie about other people. You are also not allowed to commit **fraud**. Fraud is a legal term for lying in order to get something. Although you would hopefully never commit fraud, knowing the legal terms and rules gives you information that may help you make better decisions.

What is fraud?

There are five conditions for something to be considered fraud:

1. It must be a false statement of **fact**, or lie
2. The speaker or writer must know he or she is lying
3. The speaker or writer must be trying to deceive someone
4. It must be reasonable for the victim to rely on the information
5. The victim must be harmed in some way.

Many fraud cases involve a person selling something. However, it is important to remember that certain things are allowed when selling. Let's say you go to a yard sale. Someone wants to sell you a used video game. The seller says, "This game is awesome. It's the most fun, ever." Now, even if the seller hates the game, this is not fraud. It is not fraud because calling something "awesome" and "the most fun ever" are not statements of fact. They are simply **opinions**. Even if the seller hates the game, as a seller he is allowed to try to make it seem better than he believes it to be.

Let's say the seller tells you that the game is the newest version. He doesn't know that a newer version came out last week. This is not fraud because he is not intentionally lying. If the seller tells you that within one week of playing the game, your fingers will become so strong that you can bench press 100 lbs, this is also not fraud. It is not reasonable for you to believe such an outlandish statement.

This may sound pretty silly when talking about a video game. But imagine applying this information to a large purchase, such as a house or car. It is important for you to realize that as a consumer you have a responsibility to search out as much information as possible before making a decision. Your right to information comes with a responsibility to find the information you need.

Having information at your fingertips can protect you from fraud.

The Internet and Freedom of Information

The writers of the Constitution could not have dreamed of telephones, radios, or TVs, let alone the Internet, MP3 players, and other digital forms of information. But even though we have new technology, we have the same rights to information. Sometimes it is a challenge for the law to find ways of keeping up with technology.

Communications Decency Act
It has always been difficult to reconcile the right to free expression with issues of pornography and obscenity. In 1996, the U.S. Congress passed the Communications Decency Act (CDA). The CDA was designed to keep obscene or pornographic information off the Internet, specifically out of the eyesight of minors. The Internet has only been available to commercial organizations since 1992, so in 1996 it was still fairly new.

The **Federal Communications Commission** (FCC) regulates obscene or adult content on radio and TV. This is why adult-themed shows are generally only on at night, and shows appropriate for the whole family are on earlier in the evening. However, the Internet does not fall under the FCC's control.

Information technology has changed a lot in the past 20 years, enabling information to be presented in many different ways. Even personal computers like this one built in 1999 are now outdated. But the skills of understanding the importance of information will be relevant for much, much longer.

In 2007, writers of TV shows and movies went on **strike** to achieve a better contract. Many broadcast companies re-air TV shows on the Internet. The writers wanted to make sure they were being fairly paid when their work wound up online. This is an example of how copyright and free speech issues are developing and changing.

The ACLU v Reno

In the late 1990s, the ACLU (American Civil Liberties Union) challenged the CDA in a famous case known as ACLU v Reno. This suit was brought against Janet Reno, who was Attorney General of the United States and represented the United States in the case. The Supreme Court ruled that the law was **unconstitutional**. The justices felt that it unfairly restricted the free speech of adults. Congress tried again and passed the Child Online Protection Act in 1998, and this was also struck down. The Children's Internet Protection Act was finally passed in 2000 by the Supreme Court.

Open space?

When the Internet first became public, people saw it as a new frontier for information and technology. It was thought that unlike traditional forms of publishing and broadcasting, the Internet could be open to all, with few legal restrictions. However, as the Internet becomes more and more important to business, the ideas surrounding it are changing, and new questions are arising. File-sharing sites like YouTube are bringing up issues of privacy and ownership that the founders of our country, or even the developers of the Internet, could never have imagined.

Summary

The founders of our country thought it was important for people to have access to information and the ability to speak their minds. The 21st century is considered to be the age of information. At no time in history has so much information been so easy to get. We are surrounded by information at home, in school, and in our neighborhoods. Information is found in many sources such as books, magazines, newspapers, databases, on the Internet, on boxes or cans of food, in manuals for items we purchase, and directional or advertising signs we see.

We all have questions or problems to solve. Some of these questions or problems are the result of classroom assignments. Other questions or problems are the result of our own curiosity. Everyone should be able to find the answers to questions or solutions to problems. Not everyone has the good fortune to have the same access to information. Access to information is often determined by income and location. People with a limited income may not be able to afford to purchase books and magazines. People with a limited income are not able to purchase computers or Internet access. In order to have access to information, some people must rely on public or school libraries. However, some people may not have access to such places. Some people live in very remote locations, which prohibits access to information. These locations may be so remote that the people have no running water, electricity, or phone service. Some communities do not have a public library, and some schools do not have school libraries, so the people living in these communities have limited or no access to information.

Your rights and responsibilities

Your rights to access information are protected by the laws of our government. The creators of information are also protected by laws. They are protected by copyright and trademark laws. According to these laws, you may not use information from an author or artist as your own without permission. By using quotation marks, endnotes, footnotes, and bibliographies, you are giving credit to the authors and artists who created the information you are using. When you do not give credit to the source of your information and use it as your own, this is a form of cheating called plagiarism.

While today's new technology has created new issues, your basic right to obtain information, and responsibility to use that information fairly and wisely, has not changed.

Sources of information have changed rapidly, including the ability to access it on touch screens on cell phones. Yet understanding the importance of that information and making sure it is used properly is a skill that will always be useful.

The Bill of Rights

Amendment I

Congress shall make no law respecting an establishment of religion, or prohibiting the free exercise thereof; or abridging the freedom of speech, or of the press; or the right of the people peaceably to assemble, and to petition the government for a redress of grievances.

Amendment II

A well regulated militia, being necessary to the security of a free state, the right of the people to keep and bear arms, shall not be infringed.

Amendment III

No soldier shall, in time of peace be quartered in any house, without the consent of the owner, nor in time of war, but in a manner to be prescribed by law.

Amendment IV

The right of the people to be secure in their persons, houses, papers, and effects, against unreasonable searches and seizures, shall not be violated, and no warrants shall issue, but upon probable cause, supported by oath or affirmation, and particularly describing the place to be searched, and the persons or things to be seized.

Amendment V

No person shall be held to answer for a capital, or otherwise infamous crime, unless on a presentment or indictment of a grand jury, except in cases arising in the land or naval forces, or in the militia, when in actual service in time of war or public danger; nor shall any person be subject for the same offense to be twice put in jeopardy of life or limb; nor shall be compelled in any criminal case to be a witness against himself, nor be deprived of life, liberty, or property, without due process of law; nor shall private property be taken for public use, without just compensation.

Amendment VI

In all criminal prosecutions, the accused shall enjoy the right to a speedy and public trial, by an impartial jury of the state and district wherein the crime shall have been committed, which district shall have been previously ascertained by law, and to be informed of the nature and cause of the accusation; to be confronted with the witnesses against him; to have compulsory process for obtaining witnesses in his favor, and to have the assistance of counsel for his defense.

Amendment VII

In suits at common law, where the value in controversy shall exceed twenty dollars, the right of trial by jury shall be preserved, and no fact tried by a jury, shall be otherwise reexamined in any court of the United States, than according to the rules of the common law.

Amendment VIII

Excessive bail shall not be required, nor excessive fines imposed, nor cruel and unusual punishments inflicted.

Amendment IX

The enumeration in the Constitution, of certain rights, shall not be construed to deny or disparage others retained by the people.

Amendment X

The powers not delegated to the United States by the Constitution, nor prohibited by it to the states, are reserved to the states respectively, or to the people.

Glossary

bibliography   list of sources used in researching a topic

censor   delete information

cite   list as a resource

copyright   protection given to an author or artist against copying in any form without the permission of the author or artist

democratic   related to a government controlled by the people

endnote   note placed at the end of a report that gives the source of a quote or paraphrase of information from a resource used in writing the report

fact   something that can be proven to be true

fair use   part of the copyright law that allows a person to use portions of a work for educational or other purposes without getting the creator's permission

Federal Communications Commission   U.S. government agency that oversees media communication

footnote   note placed at the bottom of the page of a report that gives the source and page of a quote or paraphrase of information from a resource used in writing the report

fraud   intentional lie told to trick someone

libel   false statement made about a person in writing that damages that person's reputation

Library Bill of Rights   policy statement by the American Library Association regarding the right of all citizens to have free access to information

online   connected to or available through a computer system

opinion   statement of belief

piracy   stealing; usually referring to copying electronic information, such as a CD or DVD

plagiarism   using the ideas or words of another person as one's own

slander   spoken false statement that damages the reputation of a person

Standards for the 21st Century Learner   set of standards developed by the American Association of School Librarians that outlines the skills students need to locate, evaluate, and use information

strike   organized stop of work so that a group of workers has more power to negotiate

Supreme Court   judicial branch of the United States government, responsible for deciding cases involving constitutional rights

unconstitutional   against the U.S. Constitution

Find Out More

Books

Gaines, Ann Graham. *Don't Steal Copyrighted Stuff*. Berkeley Heights, NJ: Enslow, 2008.

Schwartau, Winn. *Internet and Computer Ethics for Teens (and Parents and Teachers Who Haven't Got a Clue)*. Seminole, FL: Interpact Press, 2001.

Simpson, Carol. *Copyright Catechism: Practical Answers to Everyday School Dilemnas*. Columbus, OH: Linworth Books, 2005.

Teitelbaum, Michael. *The Bill of Rights*. Chanhassen, MN: The Child's World, 2005.

Websites

www.cyberbee.com/citing.html
A website primarily for educators that deals with electronic issues. This page explains how to cite Internet sources.

www.loc.gov/families
Learn more about the Library of Congress with this website.

www.splc.org/foiletter.asp
A website to help students gain access to public documents. The site also contains a section for student newspaper writers and editors.

Disclaimer

All the Internet addresses (URLs) given in this book were valid at the time of going to press. However, due to the dynamic nature of the Internet, some addresses may have changed, or sites may have changed or ceased to exist since publication. While the author and publishers regret any inconvenience this may cause readers, no responsibility for any such changes can be accepted by either the author or the publishers. It is recommended that adults supervise students on the Internet.

Further Research

Now that you know about your right to information, exercise it! Practice your research skills by researching some of the topics mentioned in this book.

Freedom of Information Act

Review the information on the Freedom of Information Act (pages 14–15). What countries do and do not have similar laws? Are any countries currently considering creating such laws?

Copyright

Review the information on famous copyright cases (pages 30–34). See if you can find copies of both "He's So Fine" and "My Sweet Lord." Do you think the two songs sound alike? What was the final decision in the J.K. Rowling case?

Fraud

Review the information on fraud (pages 38–39). Recently, several cases of literary fraud have occurred, including fake memoirs and news stories. How do these things happen? Why do people write these kinds of fake stories?

Websites

Which countries around the world grant their citizens the right to information? Which do not? What do the two groups of countries have in common?

Index

ACLU (American Civil
   Liberties Union) 39
ACLU v Reno 39
adult content 6, 13, 38
American Library
   Association 13, 22
art 24, 25, 28, 31, 40
authors 7, 25, 28, 31, 32,
   34, 40

bibliographies 33, 34, 35, 40
Bill of Rights 8, 11, 25,
   42–43
book banning 12–13
"Book Buddy" programs 7
books 4, 6, 7, 8, 12–13, 16,
   22, 24, 30, 31, 32, 33, 40
Boston Public Library 5

Carnegie, Andrew 5
censorship 11, 12, 13
censuses 20
Charity Navigator 16
Child Online Protection
   Act 39
Children's Internet
   Protection Act 39
citations 34
college libraries 7
Communications Decency
   Act (CDA) 38, 39
compact discs (CDs) 6, 31
computers 6, 16, 27, 34, 40
Constitution of the United
   States 8, 25, 38, 39, 43
consumer rights 16
copying. See plagiarism.
copyright laws 28, 30–31, 40

databases. See online
   databases.
Declaration of
   Independence 8

editors 12
elections 18, 25
e-mails 27
endnotes 34, 40

Facebook 27
facts 9, 36
fair use 28, 30–31
Federal Communications
   Commission (FCC) 38
fiction books 6, 7, 31
file-sharing websites 39
First Amendment 8, 10,
   12, 25
footnotes 33, 34, 40
Franklin, Benjamin 5
fraud 36
Freedom of Information Act
   (FOIA) 14, 15

Freedom of Information
   Advocates Network 14
freedom of speech 8–9, 10,
   11, 25, 26, 27, 36, 39, 42
freedom of the press 8, 10,
   11, 14, 42
Freedom of the Press Act
   (Sweden) 14

gossip 27
governments 4, 8, 10, 11,
   14, 16, 18, 20, 24, 25, 40

Harrison, George 28
Harry Potter books 31
Hazelwood School District v
   Kuhlmeir 11
health care 18
"He's So Fine" (song) 28
historical research 7, 14

identity theft 21, 27
"inalienable" rights 8
Internet 4, 10, 18, 24, 27,
   31, 38, 39, 40

Jefferson, Thomas 5

laws 8, 14, 18, 20, 25, 26,
   28, 30, 31, 38, 39, 40
lexicons 31
libel 9, 25, 26
libraries 4, 5, 6–7, 10, 12,
   13, 16, 22, 23–24, 40
Library Bill of Rights 22, 23
lying 36

magazines 6, 10, 12, 18,
   34, 40
medical research. See health
   care.
music 4, 18, 28, 31
MySpace 27
"My Sweet Lord" (George
   Harrison) 28

newspapers 9, 10, 11, 12,
   14, 40
note taking 33

online databases 31, 40
online social groups 16, 18
opinions 16, 18, 26, 27,
   28, 36

permission 27, 28, 40
personal papers 7
piracy 31
plagiarism 32–33, 34, 40
privacy 20, 39
problem solving 40
protests 11, 27
public libraries 4, 5, 6–7, 13,
   24, 40

publishing companies 12, 34

quotations 33, 34, 40

remote areas. See rural
   areas.
Reno, Janet 39
responsibilities 18, 25, 27,
   36, 40
reviews 18
"Right to Know Day" 14
rough drafts 33
Rowling, J.K. 31
rural areas 16, 24, 40

sampling 28
school libraries 4, 6, 12, 13,
   22, 23–24, 40
School Library Bill of Rights
   22
school newspapers 10, 11
search engines 32
September 11 attacks 14
slander 9, 25, 26
sources 18, 32, 33, 34, 35
special libraries 7
Standards for the 21st
   Century Learner 22,
   23–24
surveys 20

television 4, 10
time management 33
Tinker v Des Moines
   Independent Community
   School District 11
trademark laws 40

United Nations 20
university libraries 7
U.S. Congress 8, 20, 38,
   39, 42
U.S. Supreme Court 11, 39

Vietnam War 11
voting. See elections.

websites 4, 10, 16, 20, 27,
   31, 32, 39
Winfrey, Oprah 26–27
word-processing programs
   34

YouTube 39